Nonprofit Quick Guide™

How to Run a Strategic Planning Retreat

Linda Lysakowski, ACFRE
Joanne Oppelt, MHA

Nonprofit Quick Guide: How to Run a Strategic Planning Retreat

One of the **Nonprofit Quick Guide**™ series

Published by Joanne Oppelt Consulting, LLC

Copyright © 2021 by Joanne Oppelt and Linda Lysakowski

ISBN Print Book: 978-1-951978-16-7

13 12 11 10 9 8 7 6 5 4 3 2 1

Printed in the United States of America

About the Authors

LINDA LYSAKOWSKI, ACFRE

Linda is one of approximately one hundred professionals worldwide to hold the Advanced Certified Fundraising Executive designation. Linda is the author of ten nonfiction books and a contributing author, coeditor, and coauthor of seventeen others. She has also written six books in the fiction realm.

Linda has more than thirty years in the development field. She worked for a university and a museum before starting her own consulting firm. In her twenty-eight years as a philanthropic consultant, Linda has managed capital campaigns that have raised more than $50 million, helped hundreds of nonprofit organizations achieve their development goals, and trained more than fifty thousand development professionals in most of the fifty states of the United States as well as Canada, Mexico, Egypt, and Bermuda.

She served on the Association of Fundraising Philanthropy (AFP) Foundation for Philanthropy board and the Professional Advancement Division for AFP. She is a past president of the Eastern Pennsylvania and Sierra (Nevada) AFP chapters. She received the Outstanding Fundraiser of the Year award from the Eastern Pennsylvania, Las Vegas, and Sierra (Nevada) chapters of AFP, was honored with the Barbara Marion Award for Outstanding Service to AFP, and received the Lifetime Achievement Award from the Las Vegas AFP chapter.

Linda is a graduate of Alvernia University with majors in banking and finance as well as theology/philosophy and a minor in communications. As a graduate of AFP's Faculty Training Academy, she is a Master Teacher.

JOANNE OPPELT, MHA

Joanne, principal of Joanne Oppelt Consulting, LLC, is a seasoned rainmaker with a distinguished track record of success. During her twenty-five-plus years working in the nonprofit arena, she built or rebuilt successful fundraising departments at every stop, helping her organizations grow capacity and more effectively fulfill their missions.

She has held positions from grant writer to executive director at the nonprofits Community Access Unlimited, Caring Contact: A Listening Community, Family to Family Network of New Jersey, Christian Healthcare Center, March of Dimes Central New Jersey, Prevent Child Abuse New Jersey, and Maternal and Family Health Services. Her extensive background in a variety of work roles and organizations enables her to understand the realities and challenges nonprofit practitioners face–both internally and externally. Her success at every stop positions her to help any nonprofit, whether through her books or consulting practice, turn around its struggling fundraising operations.

Joanne is the author of four books and coauthor of twelve others. She has taught at Kean University as an Adjunct Professor in its graduate program. She is also a highly sought-after speaker and presenter.

Joanne holds a master's degree in health administration from Wilkes University, where she graduated with distinction. Her bachelor's degree is in education, with a minor in psychology.

Dedication

This book is dedicated to all the nonprofit professionals who plan their work and work their plan, and through their planning change the world.

Contents

Chapter One

A Word About Strategic Planning

Before we talk about the planning retreat, let's start by discussing why you need a plan and what steps you need to take before the planning retreat.

What Strategic Planning Is (And Isn't)

Many people think a strategic plan is a vision they have in their head for the organization. Or that it is the budget narrative that tells what you are investing in and why. Some just have a blank stare when they hear the words "strategic planning." Who needs that? We already know what we're doing, why we're doing it, and how much it will cost. Or they just groan if a board member or a funder mentions strategic planning. Or, they might say, "We did that three or four years ago, and nothing changed." Or "We're too busy putting out fires to waste time planning."

Guess what? If you had a strategic plan, you probably wouldn't have so many fires to put out every day.

A strategic plan is a roadmap, or if you prefer, the GPS (Global Positioning System), that starts with your mission and vision and then takes you step by step to achieve your vision while staying true to your mission and values. It's sort of like the turn-by-turn feature on your GPS. It tells you when you have to get ready to make a turn, if you need to reverse your direction, and even about congested traffic ahead. No, it's not magic and isn't going to solve all your problems. You can still get a flat tire, get rear-ended by surprise, or miss your turn because you weren't listening. However, a strategic plan, like a budget, is a good guideline to keep you on track! And it will prepare you for those bumps in the road.

If you've done a plan before and it didn't work, chances are you didn't do it right. Maybe the right people weren't involved, or you didn't set the right goals, or you didn't put action plans in place. We'll cover all that in this book. But first of all, don't be scared of the planning process. A strategic plan is a guideline to help keep you on track. It may not be perfect, but it's better than no plan at all.

Remember Alice in Wonderland? When she asked the Cheshire Cat which direction she should head, he asked her, "Alice, where do you want to go?" "I have no idea," was her answer. The Cheshire Cat, perhaps the first strategic planner, said to Alice, "Well, then, Alice, it doesn't matter which direction you take, you'll get there."

Don't be like Alice. Know where you are, know where you want to go, and then create a plan to get you there.

What's in a Strategic Plan

Most plans have the following components, all of which will be discussed in the chapters of this book:

- Introduction
- Rationale for planning
- Mission
- Vision
- Values
- Goals
- Objectives
- Strategies
- Action Steps
- Evaluation Measures

Why Strategic Planning?

Whether your nonprofit is small and struggling, in the middle of a growth spurt, or large and well established, you can benefit by looking at the future together as board and staff. In strategic planning, you have a unique opportunity for the board and staff to work together to envision your organization's future and determine how to get there. You can take advantage of strategic planning as a tool for changing your nonprofit's mode of functioning from "reactive to proactive." Reactive organizations wait until a crisis happens—key staff members leave, they lose a major funder, a natural catastrophe changes the way they do business—and then they scramble to survive and sometimes fail!

On the other hand, a proactive organization considers contingencies and has a Plan B (and maybe a Plan C, Plan D, and Plan E). Not that every event can be predicted. We all found that out in 2020. But a strategic plan will have measurements in place that can be adjusted when things happen to derail the best-laid plans.

And such plans help get everyone moving forward toward a common destination or vision. Strategic plans also have a positive impact on the sustainability of your organization. The Concord Leadership group produced a study showing that 46 percent of nonprofits did not have a strategic plan. This is appalling! What happens when there is no plan? Its analysis showed that nonprofits that had a written strategic plan were:

- ◆ More likely to collaborate with other nonprofits (83% vs. 76%)
- ◆ More likely to have boards open to taking calculated risks (65% vs. 51%)
- ◆ More likely to have their CEOs undergo an annual performance review (36% vs. 21%)
- ◆ More likely to have a formal process for measuring leadership effectiveness across the organization (75% vs. 50%)

And, not exactly coincidently, these plans make excellent public relations pieces for funders. They are an excellent basis for your case for support and organizational messaging. In addition, quite often, you'll notice them as a required item or reference in grant proposals for major projects. Funders know that written, updated plans indicate a good chance of success in meeting goals.

Changing from Reactive to Proactive

Everyone from fictional characters such as the Cheshire Cat in Alice in Wonderland to well-known, and even some not so well-known, thinkers of our time tell us the importance of knowing where you are going. As the Cheshire Cat told Alice, "If you don't know where you're going, it doesn't matter which path you take, you'll get there." Our favorite sage advice comes from the succinct lines of Steve Maraboli, author of *Life, the Truth, and Being Free*. He poses the thought-provoking question, "If you don't know exactly where you are going, how will you know when you get there?" And as another wise person said, "When you get to a fork in the road, take it." — Yogi Berra

What you don't want your organization to be faced with is that proverbial fork in the road and trying to take it without a directional sign to where you'll end up, going all directions at the same time. Or, as they say, fixing the plane while you're flying. In fact, one executive director compared it to flying the plane and charting the flight plan simultaneously. Ask any executive leader, or yourself, if you are one: Would you like to be in the frenetic world of fighting fires every day? Or would you prefer to look at your plan, decide what went wrong, and fix it?

We've noticed that many nonprofits have a tendency to plan and run at the same time, and, generally speaking, the results are not pretty. Quick fixes just seem to add to the pressure of accomplishing the greater good. Scrambling for a solution, wiping sweat off your brow, exhaling while you work—does that sound familiar? We hope not. We want you to get off the treadmill of constant battles with your board.

So, does your nonprofit organization need a roadmap or a GPS for navigating its future? With a substantial degree of certainty, we can say that the roadmap or GPS you've created through your strategic plan will help you discover a transformative benefit of strategic planning—knowing where you are and where you are going. But even more than providing direction and guidance, a strategic plan can take you away from the land of quick fixes and reactive management and operations to a better place characterized by proactive management in day-to-day activities.

Getting Started

So, how do you get started with strategic planning? And, do you need a retreat?

First, if you have a strategic plan already in place, start there. Review your most recent plan—have you reached your goals? If so, you need to set new ones. If not, are those goals still valid? Has your community changed? Have its needs changed? Are there new initiatives you are considering?

Assessing community needs, competitor offerings, and your own programs' effectiveness should be done before thinking about putting your next plan together. You can do these through surveys, research, personal interviews, and focus groups.

Before bringing together the key players to discuss further goals for your next plan, you need to answer all these questions, and you need to do your research. And after the retreat, there will be more work to do— getting the plan down on paper, then developing departmental action plans. And perhaps holding a follow-up retreat. (We'll cover that more in future chapters.)

When to Hold a Retreat

A retreat, or more likely several of them, is a great way to get the team working together and building consensus on goals. Usually, the first retreat is held after your task forces have completed the background research and determined where you are now and your key priorities. Don't start with the retreat—you will spend too much time rehashing past failures and explaining details that can be summarized in reports from the research team. The retreat should focus on building consensus on goals, objectives, and strategies. In the next chapter, we'll dive into the mechanics of the planning retreat(s).

A strategic plan is a necessary blueprint for your nonprofit to reach its goals. It is a guide to reach your final destination by helping you manage the forks in the road. It is not set in stone. It is a guiding document that you can revise as you experience bumps in the road. A core plan, though, is essential to have.

Wrapping It Up

◆ Strategic planning is critical for every nonprofit.

◆ The plan helps the board stay focused on strategic initiatives.

◆ The plan helps staff understand how they fit into the big picture.

◆ Before you start the next plan, review your most recent plan, if you have one.

◆ Do your homework before you start your plan—planning to plan.

◆ Bringing the key players together in a planning retreat is a critical part of the planning process.

Chapter Two

Planning to Plan

To plan the retreat, you should appoint a planning committee, planning cabinet, or task force if there is not already such a committee in place.

Committee Makeup

This group should include a few board members, the executive director, and some key staff people. If possible, someone who was involved in the last plan should serve on the committee. Institutional history is important.

The board's vice-chair or vice president typically chairs this committee and will lead the plan's implementation upon becoming chair or board president. The entire board will be involved in the planning process, but at least one or two board members should be on the planning committee. Remember that while staff will be implementing many of the plan's action steps, the board has a key role in implementing the plan, especially the parts that involve fundraising and representing the organization to the community.

We'll talk more about the facilitator's role in **Chapter Six**, but the person who will facilitate the retreat must be included in planning the date and time, the location, and the agenda.

What Does the Planning Committee Do?

This committee will first look at the previous plan if there is one. Some questions they will want to ask include:

- ◆ Were the goals in the last plan met?
- ◆ If they were met, great—we can start developing new goals.
- ◆ If they were not met, did we have too many goals or not the right goals? Are these goals still relevant?

◆ Did we have the right objectives and strategies to meet the goals?

◆ Did the various departments and committees have action plans developed from this plan so that each objective had action steps in place—who is going to do this task, when is it going to get done, and how much is it going to cost or raise if it is a fundraising task?

◆ Were there extenuating circumstances that prevented us from reaching those goals?

◆ If so, have these circumstances changed?

This committee will also be responsible for gathering information from stakeholders, including the community and any collaborators. This can be done through surveys, focus groups, or one-on-one interviews. The facilitator, if helping with the entire planning process, can help design effective evaluation tools.

Gathering information before bringing the key players together for the retreat is critical, even if you have a previous plan. Environments change, and you want your pulse on those changes—such as demographics in your community, economic challenges, and competition. You may want the groups surveyed to include:

◆ Staff members

◆ Board members

◆ Clients or users of your services

◆ Parents/family members of users of your services, especially if your clients are young people or the elderly

◆ Collaborators and other community partners

◆ Donors

◆ Funders

◆ Community leaders

These peoples will often have a good handle on the needs of the community. You may also need to gather data from sources such as:

◆ US Census Bureau

◆ Department of Labor

◆ Justice Department

◆ Department of Health and Human Services

◆ Department of Education

◆ Local Chambers of Commerce

◆ Other sources that deal with issues your organization faces

Department heads serving on the planning committee should review their departmental action plans and talk with their staff members to see what went right and what went wrong with the preceding plan. Discuss what factors affected the implementation of the preceding plan. Also, they can ask their staff members what they feel the goals for the next plan should be. All this information can be brought to the planning retreat to help set clearer, more realistic goals for the next planning cycle.

Do not make this committee too large. Usually, five people are sufficient to do the planning to plan. However, it takes a much larger group to actually execute the plan itself.

Planning to plan is sometimes the most critical piece of strategic planning. If you want your plan to work for you, make sure you engage in the preliminary planning process.

Wrapping It Up

◆ Planning to plan is critical.

◆ A small committee should be appointed to deal with this planning to plan.

◆ Start with your previous plan, if you have one.

◆ Whether or not you have a previous plan, assessing community needs before the retreat is vital.

Chapter Three

Who Should Attend the Planning Retreat?

Okay, we know what you're thinking! "Our board members are sick of retreats; they just want to get the plan done." "We cannot afford the time or money for a retreat." "We don't need a facilitator; we can do a retreat ourselves." "Do we really want to 'retreat' from our planning duties?"

A few years ago, it became quite popular to refer to the annual board retreat as a "board advance" to put a more positive spin on the process. After all, we want our board to advance, don't we, not to retreat from its duties?

Yes, we want the process to help advance our mission, vision, and programs. But we still like the term board retreat. Here's why.

The retreat transports your board and staff away from their usual meeting space. It gives them the time to really think about where the organization is going and how it will get there. It enables them to get to know each other better. So, retreat, rather than being a negative word, can be almost like a spiritual retreat—a time to take stock, be inspired, and move toward a more positive future.

Is the retreat a necessary part of the planning process? We say *yes!*

So, who gets invited to the retreat?

The Board

It is vital to have the entire board attend the retreat, if possible. The board's role is crucial in implementing the plan and ensuring everything the organization does follows the goals outlined in the plan. The only way to ensure board-member oversight and involvement is by having them involved in establishing the plan's goals and objectives in the first place. If all board members cannot attend (it is sometimes a challenge to find a time that suits everyone), make sure as many board members as possible will be present, especially officers and committee chairs. You might be able to make virtual attendance possible. In fact, you can conduct the entire retreat virtually (more about this later). And do provide each board member with the opportunity to provide input before the retreat through the survey we mentioned earlier. Board input is key to board buy-in.

Key Staff Members

Depending on your organization's size, you may not want to invite the entire staff unless yours is a tiny organization where a few staff members do it all. However, department chairs, or heads of departments, are critical. If there is a chief financial officer, director of human resources, development director, and one or more program department heads, they should attend and bring ideas from their departments. You probably don't want all staff members at the retreat. But do get their input by way of the department heads.

Likewise, you most likely will not invite collaborators, partners, donors, community leaders, and funders to attend the planning retreat. However, you should get their input by way of focus groups, surveys, or one-on-one interviews, especially in areas in which they are knowledgeable. Again, input is key to buy-in, especially important if you want the community to support you.

Once it's done, the board is responsible for the ultimate completion of the plan. Staff members implement the plan itself. Both the board and staff need to be involved in the planning to buy into the final plan.

Wrapping It Up

- ◆ All board members should be invited to the planning retreat(s).
- ◆ Key staff members should be invited to the planning retreat(s).
- ◆ Input will be gathered from key stakeholders before the retreat through surveys, focus groups, or one-on-one interviews. Results will be reported by the CEO, department heads, or board members.
- ◆ You can do your research virtually and can even hold the retreat(s) virtually.

Chapter Four

Where and When Should You Hold the Retreat?

Now, let's get into the meat of the retreat itself, starting with how long it should last:

A retreat should last as long as you need!

Okay, that might be too broad an answer. We find that most groups require at least two sessions to get everything done. Some groups opt for a two-day retreat, maybe a Friday evening from 5 p.m. to 9 p.m., with dinner, and Saturday morning from 8 a.m. to 1 p.m., with lunch.

Others do an intensive all-day retreat, perhaps all day on Saturday if most board members cannot get away during the week. Sometimes you need to plan several retreats over a few weeks to let the information sink in and for the facilitator to prepare a report and set the agenda for the second retreat.

Ideally, the first session is held to solidify the mission, vision, and values and determine goals. After enabling the planning cabinet/committee to review what was accomplished at the first session, a second session is held a few weeks later. Sometimes even a third session is necessary.

Where and When Should the Retreat be Held?

A retreat should be precisely what the name implies—a getaway from your regular routine—a place to step back and look at your organization with fresh eyes. Timing will depend on board and staff members' schedules and possibly other stakeholder groups you might want to invite to at least part of your retreat. You may, for example, want to invite community members to come in and help you conduct the SWOT analysis (more about this in **Chapter Five**). Fresh eyes and fresh ideas from people not intimately connected to your organization help shed light on areas you might not think are important but which the community feels are vital aspects of your programs.

One organization that served adults with developmental disabilities, for example, invited parents of the people they served to come in and talk about what they saw as the strengths, weaknesses, opportunities, and threats of the organization. The input of these parents was invaluable in helping the organization craft its plan.

Important: do not attempt to do planning at a regular board meeting. There are too many other business items that need attention and too many distractions, such as board members arriving late, leaving early, staff members being sidetracked by routine office duties, and staff being interrupted by other staff members.

If yours is a national or international organization, scheduling might be a bit more challenging. We've been involved with several national and international groups that held a special planning session before one of their regular board meetings. Getting people together for another special session would be challenging due to costs and travel time. However, with many groups, especially statewide, regional, national, and international organizations, the meetings are done virtually. This can help cut down on costs and ensure that key people can attend.

Location, Location, Location

If you are meeting in person, where do you hold your retreat? As we've said, not in your office, please!!! We've held retreats in interesting locations, such as:

- a museum
- a country club
- a bird sanctuary
- a board member's office suite
- an environmental center
- an arboretum
- a hotel
- poolside at a board member's home

As part of the retreat, you could plan an outing and invite spouses of staff and board members to attend. One group, for example, held its retreat at a museum and asked the museum director to take the participants and their spouses on a private tour of the museum afterward. Another group arranged a tour of local historic sites for spouses while the board and staff were tied up in the retreat, and then everyone had dinner together. Offering activities like this helps keep the atmosphere friendly and informal.

Holding a Virtual Retreat

Virtual retreats are becoming more popular and can be cost-effective while ensuring better attendance. If your organization is national, international, statewide, or regional, it will be easier to get them all together in a virtual setting. We've learned during the COVID-19 pandemic that people often prefer virtual meetings to avoid travel and health risks. Almost everyone is now proficient in Zoom and similar online tools that can be used. And the expenses of employing a facilitator who is not local can be significantly reduced. Although there are distinct advantages to meeting in person, such as interacting on a more personal level and side-stepping technical challenges, these can often be offset by having full participation virtually.

If you plan a virtual retreat, make sure everyone is familiar with the medium you plan to use. We find that Zoom is easy to use for most people, and you can divide people into breakout rooms for brainstorming sessions, share screens, use PowerPoint and other tools, and use whiteboards for people to make notes.

Make sure you, your board, and your team get away from the day-to-day details of their work. Make the retreat special in some way, even if you do it virtually. Set an atmosphere where people can be fully involved in the task at hand.

Wrapping It Up

- ◆ Decide how many retreat sessions you will need—usually, you need at least two sessions.
- ◆ Do not hold the retreat at your office; get away to somewhere with no distractions.
- ◆ Poll the board and staff for the most convenient time to hold your retreats.
- ◆ Virtual retreats are becoming more popular and can be cost-effective while ensuring better attendance.
- ◆ If you're using virtual retreats, make sure everyone can access the tools you are using.

Chapter Five

Setting the Agenda

What needs to covered at the retreat? Here is a typical agenda:

- ◆ Review of the previous plan
- ◆ Review of stakeholder input
- ◆ SWOT analysis
- ◆ Confirming mission, vision, and values
- ◆ Establishing goals
- ◆ Setting objectives for goals
- ◆ Brainstorming objectives and strategies
- ◆ Planning for the action plan
- ◆ Discussion of how the plan will be evaluated
- ◆ Finalizing the plan

As we've mentioned, this usually takes more than one retreat—usually two, maybe even three meetings. The facilitator and the planning committee should determine how long each retreat will be and how many sessions are needed. One way to divide this up might be:

Session One:

- ◆ Review of the previous plan
- ◆ Review of stakeholder input
- ◆ SWOT Analysis
- ◆ Confirming mission, vision, and values
- ◆ Establishing goals

Session Two:
- ◆ Setting objectives for goals
- ◆ Brainstorming objectives and strategies
- ◆ Planning for the action plan
- ◆ Discussion of how the plan will be evaluated
- ◆ Finalizing the plan

Another way to break it up, depending on how long the discussions in each area are predicted to run:

Session One:
- ◆ Review of the previous plan
- ◆ Review of stakeholder input
- ◆ SWOT Analysis
- ◆ Confirming mission, vision, and values

Session Two:
- ◆ Establishing goals
- ◆ Setting objectives for goals
- ◆ Brainstorming objectives and strategies

Session Three:
- ◆ Planning for the action plan
- ◆ Discussion of how the plan will be evaluated
- ◆ Finalizing the plan

There is no one right solution for every organization. For example, if this is your organization's first strategic plan, there will be no past plan to review so you will skip that part. But perhaps you will have more research to do, and thus the discussion on stakeholder feedback may take longer for you.

The SWOT Analysis

The SWOT analysis usually takes some explanation on the part of the facilitator. SWOT stands for strengths, weaknesses, opportunities, and threats.

Many people get confused by the differences between strengths and opportunities and the difference between weaknesses and threats. The explanation is quite simple. Strengths and weaknesses are internal to the organization. A strong executive director or a weak board are examples of strengths and weaknesses. A new company or foundation in your community might be an opportunity, while the loss of government funding is a threat.

Resist the temptation to just list things like "We have a great board" as an asset. The more specific you are, the better off you'll be. How is the board great, and how does this help the organization? A better way of putting it might be "Our board has a diversity of skills and talents useful to the organization" or "Our board members are passionate about our mission and use this passion to assist in fundraising efforts."

Also, sometimes something can be both a strength and a weakness—for example, "We have a great software system" might be listed as a strength; however, a weakness might be "No one is adequately trained to use our software." The same is true about opportunities and threats—the threat of government funding loss might present an opportunity to raise more money from private foundations, businesses, and individuals.

If your stakeholder analysis included questions about the strengths, weaknesses, opportunities, and threats, and if your departmental feedback includes these suggestions, the process might not take as long as starting from scratch. Likewise, if you have a previous plan that included a SWOT analysis, you can start with that and discuss which of these strengths and opportunities are still valid and which weaknesses and threats no longer exist. Then you can move on to develop new items in each area. The SWOT analysis is important because it helps you determine and prioritize goals.

Other evaluation methods can be done, such as appreciative inquiry and SWOTR Analysis (adding resources to the mix). We find that the SWOT analysis is still the most valid way to analyze your organization internally. But remember to use some customer-focused analysis, such as surveys, focus groups, and interviews. While your plan is internally driven, it should always focus on community needs and how you are meeting those needs.

We will discuss setting goals and objectives and the next steps in the planning process in future chapters.

Wrapping It Up

- ◆ Each step in the planning process takes time. The amount of anticipated time will vary according to your past planning process and other factors unique to your organization.
- ◆ Your agenda might include two or more retreats, depending on these factors.

◆ The SWOT analysis should be done early in the retreat process, just after reviewing the prior plan and performing stakeholder analysis.

Chapter Six

Who Facilitates the Retreat?

Engage a facilitator for your retreat who is *not* a staff or board member. Board and staff members need to have input into the planning process and will not be free to do so if they are engaged in facilitating the process.

There are other issues, as well, to be considered. For example, a staff member who leads the process may pay more attention to the things that pertain to the department in which they are employed. Even the executive director may prioritize the things that have the most importance to himself or herself.

The same is true if a board member facilitates your retreat. That board member may be involved in a committee whose work will receive more attention because it is the area this board member is most comfortable with or feels is a higher priority.

In addition to these issues, there are always personality issues to deal with. Staff members may have preconceived ideas about another staff member or that person's department. They may not see the value of conversation focused on others, even if the facilitating staff member is impartial. Perceptions count. And whether it's a board or staff member, there will always be someone who does not respect this person or value their skills even if they are an experienced facilitator.

Working with an Outside Facilitator

Bringing in an outside facilitator is always recommended. An experienced facilitator will know how to keep things on track, will be able to diffuse any uncomfortable situation that might arise among staff and board members, and is not there because he or she needs to be liked by the participants. They will be experienced in bringing all participants into the conversation, avoiding any rambling or unproductive discussions, and explaining the plan and research's nuances, such as those we already pointed out regarding the SWOT analysis.

So, you might be asking, where do we find a facilitator, and how much do they charge?

First, we suggest talking to other nonprofits in your community who have done strategic planning if you don't already have someone who helped with your previous planning needs. Ask the other nonprofits who they used and how satisfied they were with the result. Also, ask about the facilitator's personality and style. As with any consultant you engage, find one that suits your organizational personality. Some board and staff members will want a no-nonsense person who gets right to the heart of the planning process, and others prefer a more casual but still professional approach.

Of course, before you talk to planning consultants, be sure you know what you need them to do. Especially if this is the first time you've gone through the planning process, you might need a consultant that can guide you every step of the way, from selecting your planning committee, reviewing previous plans, doing the research—perhaps designing surveys and conducting focus groups or maybe just pointing you in the right direction to accomplish these things yourself. Do you want the consultant to actually prepare the planning document, or will you do that yourself? If you are experienced at this process, you may just want someone to facilitate the retreat(s) for you. We tend to find that most organizations want someone who can "do it all," from the research to writing the plan. But look at your skills, your budget, and your available time to determine what is the best solution for you.

Once you know what you want, you can either prepare a formal request for proposal (RFP) or put the job out to bid. You can send the RFP to consultants you've identified through your networks by searching the Internet or researching referrals from professional organizations. When you compare prices, be sure you are also comparing the scope of work being proposed.

Choose the Right Facilitator

One word of caution. When selecting someone to help with your planning needs, talk to people who have experience with nonprofits and are familiar with the differences in strategic planning for nonprofits and strategic planning for businesses.

Business consultants typically don't have experience in nonprofit governance and fundraising. With regard to governance, large corporations have board members, but their role is different from that of a nonprofit board. Fundraising, in particular, is an area businesses do not need to worry about because of the way they generate income. And while revenue is essential to companies, they are not a public trust seeking donations like a nonprofit organization.

One nonprofit where Linda worked was offered "free services" from a strategic planner employed to do strategic planning in a large financial institution. While he was good at his job, he was not experienced in strategic planning for a nonprofit, and the resulting plan did not touch on either nonprofit governance or fundraising. And, frankly, board governance and fundraising are the two most significant areas of focus for most of the nonprofit strategic planning retreats we've done.

Your consultant will work with you to develop a timeline and a budget, plan the agendas for the retreat(s), and, depending on the scope of work for which you have engaged the consultant, will conduct the research, and create the written planning document for your approval.

If your organization is on a tight budget and cannot afford a planning consultant, you may be able to barter with another nonprofit CEO to facilitate your retreat. Or you could find a volunteer, perhaps through SCORE (the Service Corps of Retired Executives, https://www.score.org) or your local university. But again, be certain that this person has experience with nonprofits and their unique issues.

Wrapping It Up

- ◆ Always use an outside facilitator for your retreat, and most often, for the entire planning process.
- ◆ Determine the scope of work before you start talking to consultants.
- ◆ Ask other nonprofits, search professional organizations, and search the Internet and talk to several consultants before making your decision.
- ◆ Always look for a facilitator/consultant experienced in the nonprofit sector.

Chapter Seven

Confirming or Establishing Mission, Vision, and Values

One of the important things to accomplish at your retreat is reviewing and, if necessary, changing your mission, vision, and values documents. These are important documents that should control everything your organization does, and your goals must conform to your mission, vision, and values. Even if you don't make changes, review your mission, vision, and value statements at the beginning of the retreat, so they are foremost in participants' minds.

Your Mission

Although it is often too lengthy, too wordy, not up to date, or not conforming with your values, most organizations have a mission statement.

Clarifying your mission statement may be as easy as saying yes; the mission statement adequately describes the organization's overall purpose. On the other hand, you may decide to integrate new elements or delete elements that no longer apply. Periodically, the IRS audits nonprofits on conformance to their chartering documents. We have known nonprofits that have gotten into trouble because their current activities did not promote the agency's mission as stated in its formation or amended formation documents. Make sure that when you plan, you stick to your mission.

Your mission should concisely and accurately explain:

◆ Why does your organization exist?

◆ Who does the organization serve?

◆ What makes the organization unique?

◆ What is the organization most noted for in the community?

Your mission statement should be a specific, succinct articulation of what stakeholders wish your organization to be. What about the wording of the mission statement?

Examples of Concise Mission Statements

◆ Make-A-Wish Foundation: We serve a unique and vital role in helping to strengthen and empower children battling life-threatening medical conditions.

◆ Charity Water: We're a nonprofit organization bringing clean, safe drinking water to people in developing countries.

◆ Livestrong Foundation: We unite, inspire, and empower people affected by cancer.

◆ Mt. Laurel Library (NJ): We inform, enrich, connect, and transform our community.

◆ Alexander Dawson School challenges its students to achieve excellence of mind, body, and character through a rigorous college-preparatory program.

Your Vision for the Future

The vision statement for your organization may seem lofty; the purpose of the vision, after all, is to inspire both the community and the clients. The vision describes your organization's preferred future state or what the organization wants to be in the future. You will want your vision to focus not just on how you see your organization in the future but also on your vision for your community.

A good vision statement answers the question, "What would a perfect world look like?" or "What would a world that no longer needs our organization look like?"

Some questions you might ask regarding your vision statement include:

◆ What are the ultimate goals we are trying to achieve (i.e., end hunger, cure a disease, have a well-educated population, save a river?)

◆ What do we want our community to look like (i.e., free from violence, creative, strong workforce, a great place to live?)

If you don't already have viable mission, values, and vision statements, this needs to be done before you can complete your plan.

Examples Of Good Vision Statements:

◆ Feeding America: A hunger-free America.

◆ Oceana: We seek to make our oceans as rich, healthy, and abundant as they once were.

◆ San Diego Zoo: To become a world leader at connecting people to wildlife and conservation.

Values

Your values statements are your "line in the sand." These are the things you hold dear and will not compromise on. Many organizations, we find, have mission statements but fall short on defining their vision and values. Every organization has different values, but here are some examples of things that might be important to your organization. If you have a values statement, review it at the retreat. If not, this is a good time to develop one. Your values might include things such as:

◆ Openness

◆ Caring

◆ Integrity

◆ Diversity

◆ Quality

◆ Transparency

◆ Inclusiveness

◆ Equity

◆ Knowledge

Your mission, vision, and values statement define who your nonprofit is, what it's working toward, and how it conducts itself. All foundational statements to have before you engage in setting goals for the plan.

Wrapping It Up

◆ If you already have mission, vision, and values statements, plan a review of them at the beginning of the retreat.

◆ Understand the difference between mission, vision, and value statements.

◆ Brevity is best. "Less is more."

◆ All your goals must reflect your mission, vision, and values.

◆ If you are lacking in any of these documents, this is the time to create them.

◆ Creating a new mission, vision, and values will take more time, so be sure to allow adequate time on your agenda to discuss these items.

Chapter Eight

Setting Goals

Ah, the crux of the retreat—goal setting. This is typically a portion of the agenda that you will spend a lot of time on. When doing your goal setting, remember these few basic terms and concepts.

- ◆ The plan will have overall goals (such as creating more awareness of your organization in the community, building a stronger board, expanding services to particular populations, or adding more services for existing clients).
- ◆ Goals are broad-based and often hard to measure because they are lofty and overarching.
- ◆ Every goal must have measurable objectives (we often call these objectives SMART—they must be specific, measurable, action-oriented, realistic, and time-defined).
- ◆ Strategies answer the question, "How are we going to achieve our objectives and, as a result, our goals?"
- ◆ Strategic plans must be translated into departmental work plans, which include timelines, areas of responsibility, and budgets.

Setting Goals

So, how do you start to establish goals? First, let's start at the beginning. If you have a previous plan you are working with, review those goals—have they been met? If you're still working on them—should you be, and are they still valid goals? Look at your stakeholder input—are there new goals you should be thinking about, and are you really the right organization to tackle these goals? Should you be partnering or collaborating with other organizations to meet community needs?

Then there is the age-old question—how many goals can we handle? There is no magic answer. Every organization is different, but in general, we feel that three to five main goals are enough for most organizations. So, if your board and staff are suggesting fifteen or twenty goals, take a look at this and have some serious discussion on things like:

◆ Are these really goals, or are they objectives to help you reach a broader goal?

◆ Can some of these goals be combined into one?

◆ Is it realistic to think we have the resources to achieve these goals, or get to them all?

◆ Are these goals immediate, or can they be deferred—in other words, are they must do's, should do's, or it would be nice to do's?

◆ Are the goals to be accomplished this year or sometime in the future?

Establishing Objectives

Once you've defined your top priority goals and reached a consensus, you can start to develop the objectives and strategies that will help you achieve your goals. For example, let's take a goal of "creating more awareness of your organization in the community." You might have several objectives to help you attain that goal. Knowing that goals, such as creating awareness, are often difficult to measure, the objectives must be measurable. Some objectives for this goal, for example, might include things like:

◆ We will update our website to make it more user-friendly and gain more followers by June 30, 20xx.

◆ We will develop better media relationships by creating, and delivering to key media contacts, media kits by August 31, 20xx.

◆ We will issue press releases monthly beginning July 1, 20xx.

◆ We will conduct monthly cultivation events during the 20xx fiscal year and thereafter.

As you can see, these objectives have specific actions associated with them, are measurable, are action-oriented (they involve doing something), are realistic based on the budget and human resources that will be required, and are time-defined.

On the other hand, strategies deal with the "how" you are going to accomplish the objectives. For example, updating your website might include strategies such as appointing a task force to review other nonprofit websites and determining what features you like and don't like, engaging a professional website designer, gathering client stories from staff and getting photo permissions to include on your website, and establishing a means to accept donations if you don't already have that feature on your website. Your specific strategies will differ based on your organizational capacity, processes, and procedures.

At the retreat, it will be important that the facilitator explain the terminology of goals, objectives, and strategies to your participants, and facilitate the participants to work as a team, often in small groups, to create specific goals, objectives, and strategies. Terminology can often be confusing to people who are new to the planning process.

Wrapping It Up

- ◆ Goals are broad-based and often not easily measured.
- ◆ Objectives must be developed for each goal.
- ◆ Objectives must be SMART—specific, measurable, action-oriented, and time-defined.
- ◆ Strategies answer the "how" you are going to accomplish your objectives.

Chapter Nine

Brainstorming

Brainstorming is an important part of your retreat. No one wants to listen to a facilitator lecture, or an executive director tell them how the organization will operate, or staff complain, or board members question everything the staff is doing. Strategic planning is a team effort, and it's essential to work as a team.

Remember that the term brainstorming implies that you throw out ideas, rationally discuss them, and sift through the results, selecting those ideas that seem like they have the most potential. There are no "dumb ideas." Even though sometimes you get some wild, innovative ideas, these ideas may often spark something that, when modified, could be viable.

Some instances where brainstorming as a group will help:

◆ Confirming or revising the mission, vision, and values

◆ Doing the SWOT analysis

◆ Setting goals

Brainstorming Opportunities

You may not want to get into wordsmithing mission statements and vision statements, but you can brainstorm and develop the keywords and phrases that the group agrees on. Then appoint a person, or a small group, to propose a final statement that the group can vote on by email or at the next retreat.

The SWOT analysis is a good place for brainstorming, too. Some of the ideas may be mentioned under the wrong categories, may be redundant, or may not be agreed upon by the entire group. However, a good facilitator will guide you through this process. The main thing is for everyone to feel that their voice is heard. One of the things we've noticed is that it is easy to start out with strengths because everyone likes to talk about the good things in their organization, whereas sometimes weaknesses take a little more "tooth-pulling" because people don't want to talk about the bad stuff. A good facilitator will be able to get this ball rolling.

Goal setting is also a good time for brainstorming. Usually, there are too many goals to tackle all at once, and the goals need to be prioritized. The best way to decide which goals you need to include in your plan is to 1) review past goals, 2) review the SWOT analysis, and 3) consider the input you've received from stakeholders through surveys, focus groups, or interviews. Goals must be agreed upon by both the board and staff. If you have too many goals, the facilitator can guide the group through the process of reviewing all the suggested goals, determine if any are redundant or can be combined into one, clarify if it is a goal or if it is an objective that falls under a stated goal, and determine if it a realistic goal for this plan or should be placed in a "parking lot" for discussion.

Sometimes it is good to break the group into smaller groups for brainstorming. This is especially helpful during the first discussion of goal setting and during the objective setting phase. Goals can be discussed in small groups, and then the whole group comes together to prioritize and clarify them.

Once the goals are finalized, small groups can then be assigned to come up with objectives to meet these goals. Let's say, for example, the group agrees that the final goals should be:

◆ Raising community awareness of the organization
◆ Becoming less dependent on government funding
◆ Expanding our programs into two more counties
◆ Increasing the board's involvement in marketing and fundraising

You might then split the large group into four smaller groups, each one focusing on one of these goals and coming up with objectives for that particular goal. When you split the groups for goal setting, they can be random, but we suggest that when the smaller groups focus on establishing objectives, you have the right people involved in each group.

In the example above, the first small group should include the marketing staff, the board's marketing committee if there is one, or perhaps some board members who are experts in, or have expressed interest in, this area. The second group could include the chief development officer, any members of the development committee on the board, and people who have expertise or interest in fundraising. The third group should include program staff, any board members who live or work in those countries or have a knowledge of them, and any board members who have an interest in the programs in question. The final group might include the board chair, the executive director, and any staff or board members interested in these areas.

As we've said, brainstorming is essential because it keeps the participants actively engaged, enthused, and maybe even awake! It also makes everyone—board and staff members—understand that their input is important and their participation in implementing the plan critical. And no one feels that someone else's ideas are more important than theirs or that certain ideas will be forced on the group.

Wrapping It Up

◆ Brainstorming helps everyone stay engaged in the process.

◆ There are no "dumb ideas," just maybe ideas that need refining or delaying until a better time.

◆ Some brainstorming should do with the group as a whole— mission, vision, values, and SWOT analysis.

◆ Goal setting can be done by the entire group or by small breakout groups who then come together as a whole group.

◆ Establishing objectives is often one area in which small groups that include the experts in those areas can work effectively, and then bring back their ideas to the entire group.

Chapter Ten

After the Retreat

Whew, congratulations! Your retreat is over. Now what?

Well, you still have to develop your written plan. And make sure you have departmental action plans that will ensure that the overall plan gets implemented. If you've been working with a consultant to plan and facilitate your retreat, this person is often the one to prepare the final plan. If your planning committee members chose to do this internally, they would probably be the ones to put the final plan together. Whichever route you choose, you need a written plan. We strongly believe in the adage that it never happened and never will if it isn't written down.

The Written Plan

Some organizations will prepare the written plan with the basics. Usually, the outline goes like this:

- Mission
- Vison
- Values
- Agency Description
- Background of the Planning Process
- Background Research
- SWOT Analysis
- Goals
- Objectives
- Reference to the Action Plans
- Evaluation techniques
- Names of the People Involved in the Planning Process

◆ Appendix Showing Surveys/Focus Group Questions/Interview Questions Used in Gathering Information

Other organizations may include the action steps in the planning document. Action plans should be done for various departments within the organization. These typically include:

◆ Program Plan (may include more than one if your organization has several programs)

◆ Development/Fundraising Plan

◆ Facilities Plan (especially if you have a large facility complex)

◆ Financial Plan

◆ Board Development Plan

Action plans must be detailed. Every objective should have specific action steps that will show how these objectives will be implemented and measured. The action steps must answer three questions:

◆ Who is responsible for this action step?

◆ When is it going to begin and end?

◆ How much will it cost and/or how much money will it bring into the organization?

In other words, you will have columns for the person or group responsible for each action step, a starting and ending date for this step to be accomplished, and the budget (positive and negative).

Using these steps, you can easily develop measurements that will be used to measure progress. Is the task on budget? Is it being done on time? Do you have the people necessary to accomplish this step, and do they have the tools they need to get it done? Often when preparing planning documents, we include lists for each person/department/group of the tasks they are responsible for. And we include a chronological timeline for accomplishing the plan and a budget showing expected income and expenses. This is the best way to measure the plan. Each person or department can measure their progress, and the person or team in charge of the plan can measure overall progress and suggest corrections to the plan if things are not moving according to schedule.

Finetuning the Plan

Once you see the action plans laid out, you will know if the plan is realistic or if you need to make adjustments. We all know that "stuff happens." A person responsible for a task leaves or goes on an extended absence. The timeline cannot be realistically accomplished by the established deadline. Budget cuts may happen mid-year due to unforeseen circumstances (many faced this in 2020). Don't forget—your plan is a guideline; it is not set in stone. But regular measurement and evaluation will allow you to make corrections midstream instead of waiting until the plan's term is over.

Once you have the final plan, it is crucial to operationalize it through departmental action plans. And use those action plans as measures of progress. Make your strategic plan a living, breathing document. The plan will do you no good sitting on a shelf gathering dust.

Wrapping It Up

◆ Don't forget the importance of capturing everything in a written document.

◆ Departments will each develop their own action plans.

◆ The action steps will help measure success.

◆ The plan is not written in stone—it is a guideline—remember that "stuff happens."

Chapter Eleven

Bringing It All Together

So, now you should not only be ready to plan your planning retreat(s), but you will know what needs to happen before and after. The planning process is a complex one, and we could talk a lot more about things like getting input from stakeholders and putting the written plan together. Hopefully, you have chosen a facilitator for your planning retreat to help you with the other steps.

It is usually difficult to do the entire plan yourself, but it is imperative that you use an outside facilitator for the retreat(s). As we've said, usually there are at least two retreats needed to accomplish everything that has to be done.

However, don't be intimidated by the amount of work, time, and money that goes into this process. You will come out of this with a product and a process for all your planning efforts. And both staff and board will take ownership of the plan because they helped create it. When the right people are not involved in the planning, they are usually reluctant to help implement the plan.

The plan can help you convince funders that you know what you're doing, have put community needs at the forefront of your work, and have an engaged board and staff.

As you can see, the plan is both a process and product; both are important. We've talked here mostly about process, but the final product is critical, too. You can learn more about both the product and the process through Linda's course, "Nonprofit Strategic Planning: Do It Right," available at https://lindalysakowski.com.

And remember, if you need help with your plan, you can contact either of us: Linda@LindaLysakowski.com or Joanne@joanneoppelt.com.

Happy planning!